SCORPIO

HOROSCOPE

& ASTROLOGY

2020

Scorpio

Horoscope & Astrology

2020

Published by Mystic Shores publications

Suite SM-2380-6403

14601 North Bybee Lake Court

Portland, Oregon 97203

Phone: +1 (805) 308-6503

islandauthor@hotmail.com

Acknowledgment:

Thank you to the stargazers, dreamers, and mystics. You make this world a better place.

SCORPIO 2020 OVERVIEW

The stars align favorably for Scorpio in 2020. Inspiration and innovation come out in front, encouraging new ideas and concepts which inspire growth. Not one, not two, not three, but four Supermoons in 2020 ensures plenty of emotional water energy arrives to encourage Scorpio to develop their dreams in tune with their passion and heart. Scorpio is in their element during this time. There is astonishing progress to be made in 2020, Scorpio utilizes the power of the water to make progress on their most substantial goals.

Mercury Retrograde is the most significant destabilizing force in 2020. Forewarned is forearmed and Scorpio does find that bridges can be burnt if not handled sensitively. Being mindful of interpersonal relationships during the retrograde phase allows Scorpio to forge a delicate path through these troublesome cosmic storms. Scorpio can harness the emotional power of their star sign to find solutions and take an affirmative action before relationships steer off course.

2020 is a year which blends the elemental forces of Earth, Air, Fire, and Water with new world technology. This dramatically expands the Scorpio star signs intuitive abilities. The star sign Scorpio is one of water dominance, and when harnessed correctly, Scorpio makes remarkable progress as they light the path forward toward their emotional goals. Compassionate and idealistic endeavors abound for Scorpio in this most incredible year of potentiality.

With so many compelling reasons to shine, the star sign Scorpio can look forward to incredible cosmic energy, which helps increase and boost their potential possible in 2020, and beyond.

Scorpio

Scorpio Dates: October 23 to November 21
Symbol: Scorpion
Element: Water
Planet: Mars, Pluto
House: Eighth
Colors: Red, black

JANUARY ASTROLOGY

January 3 – First Quarter Moon in Aries.

This Moon phase occurs at 04.45 UTC.

January 3, 4 - Quadrantids Meteor Shower.

The Quadrantids meteor shower run yearly from January 1-5. The Quadrantids meteor shower peaks this year on the night of the 3rd and morning of the 4th.

January 10 - Full Moon in Cancer.

This full moon phase occurs at 19:21 UTC. This full moon is called the Full Wolf Moon because this was the time of year when hungry wolf packs howled outside camps. This full moon has also been known as the Old Moon and the Moon After Yule.

January 10 - Penumbral Lunar Eclipse.

A penumbral lunar eclipse occurs as the Moon passes through the Earth's partial shadow or penumbra. During this type of eclipse, the Moon will darken slightly but won't wholly eclipse. This penumbral eclipse is visible throughout most of Europe, Africa, Asia, and Western Australia.

January 17 – Last Quarter Moon in Libra.

This Moon phase occurs at 12.58 UTC.

January 24 – New Moon in Capricorn.

This new moon phase occurs at 21:42 UTC. The Moon is on the same side of the Earth as the Sun and will not be visible in the night sky. This phase occurs at 21:03 UTC. This is an excellent time to view galaxies and stars as there is no moonlight to obscure your view of the universe.

JANUARY HOROSCOPE

JANUARY WEEK ONE

You are ready to stir up mischief and find an adventurous path to travel down. There is a restlessness within your spirit, which seeks self-expression. It is a beautiful calling that helps you move out of your comfort zone and discover new opportunities. This is a pivotal time to focus on expanding your social circle, staying open to invitations to mingle, does create the right conditions to enjoy a lively chapter. A vital plan set in motion can reach fruition. It enables more security and abundance to flow into your life. You can harness the power of an essential opportunity to steady your foundations and create a wellspring of stability from which to grow your goals. This shines the spotlight on planning long-term goals, you can take the decisive actions needed to create a successful result. You can cast your net wide during this expansive phase. Potential is soaring through your life, and this may well inspire you to broaden your reach of what you thought was possible. It does lead to a fantastic phase of growth as you embark on an adventure which sees you explore life possibilities. This is a time which enables you to draw in visionary ideas which speak to your soul. You find a new landscape is creating forward momentum in your social life. It is a time of lively discussions and thoughtfulness. You do explore the broader world of potential around you, this does involve a more social environment, you connect with people whose thoughts and ideas complement yours. It is a beautiful time for being around kindred spirits. It does help move you forward towards a happier chapter.

JANUARY WEEK TWO

This week speaks of matters close to your home and heart, rich traditions which have combined beautifully with new approaches that you have made your own. The better you build your environment, the better the foundation for you to propel your dreams from. There is magic to be made by staying right to your heart, you are drawing opportunities into your life, it does facilitate a shift towards abundance and happiness as more treasured memories are created. It does put creative matters on the front burner and cranks up the heat of visionary ideas. Sifting through your options allows you to pick the ripest fruit. You may discover a new mentor who is established in a field, you are curious about. This one can give you candid feedback on the potential possible. It is a stellar time to pitch a new enterprise forward, it may lead to fascinating long-term goals coming into view. You're still finding your way, but you will come into your own soon. It will bring you a sense of accomplishment, and get you on track with building your own personal empire. Reconfiguring your goals and fine-tuning your energy does deliver the most essential outcomes in your life. Focusing on a daily routine which will be especially helpful in creating those actions which stabilize your foundations. Your life is set to lighten up. Ditching other commitments and demands that drain your energy down does refresh your spirit and enables you to discover leads which inspire your mind and lead to growth. It is an entire chapter for creating space for a new adventure. You can expand those horizons into an avenue which offers you a room to progress your skills. It is a time of exciting projects and heightened creativity.

JANUARY WEEK THREE

There is plenty of positive energy coming, which shines a light on an optimistic chapter. It does have you feeling excited about a new adventure. A lofty plan is set into motion, it is an ideal time where you can give your goals a fantastic boost. The power to generate positive results is exceptionally reliable during this incredible time. You certainly can plan to achieve excellent outcomes. As you plant the seeds for a new adventure, you can dare to expand your horizons. You manifest a vision which emanates from your subconscious mind. This venture raises your level of joy and inspiration, as you discover a path which is in alignment with your emotional being. An offer arrives to tempt you into the broader community, and this sees your energy attracting people who merge well with your thoughts, leading to lively discussions. Engaging in activities that make your heart sing does help the abundance flow into your world. It does raise your levels of joy and bring you in contact with the right kind of individual. This is someone you can connect well with, friendship blossoms through the sharing of thoughts, ideas, and experiences. It does give you a much-needed boost and offers you a chance to develop a meaningful bond.

JANUARY WEEK FOUR

You may be craving more security in your life, if you have been feeling intense, know that your circumstances are set to improve. You can gather your resources and forge ahead towards the development of a goal, giving you a decisive victory. A creative project is likely to take off for you. You are best to look at your options, as sorting through your goals and possibilities will help you get a clearer picture of an area that can be developed. There may be a path you have been considering which can be exciting, but it can also feel daunting to move in a new direction. You have what it takes to revolutionize your situation and draw positive outcomes. You have dealt with considerably tricky circumstances, and she is proud of the way you have grown into a resilient and capable person. A turning point is reached soon, and this heralds the beginning of a fresh start, which is gentle and more optimistic. This week reveals a silver lining, which clears the decks for you soon. You see yourself moving in a more balanced direction, it does bring more harmony into your life, and this is a shift which draws abundance into your life to create more stability on the homefront. You have many possibilities at your disposal for personal growth, it's a beautiful time to focus on a relevant area. You have valuable gifts to share, you may even launch an exciting project or online venture which celebrates your talents. You are ready to crack open a new chapter and expand your horizons in an area which offers you significant advancement.

FEBRUARY ASTROLOGY

February 2 – First Quarter Moon in Taurus. This Moon phase occurs at 1.42 UTC.

February 9 - Full Moon in Leo, Supermoon.

The Moon is on the opposite side of the Earth as the Sun and will be fully illuminated. This phase occurs at 7:33 UTC. This full moon is known as the Full Snow Moon because the heaviest snows usually fall during this month. Since hunting is difficult, this full moon has also been recognized as the Full Hunger Moon, since the harsh weather made fishing difficult. This is the first of four supermoons for 2020. The Moon will be at its nearest approach to the Earth and will look slightly larger and brighter than usual.

February 10 - Mercury at largest Eastern Elongation.

The planet Mercury reaches an eastern elongation of 18.1 degrees from the Sun.

February 15 – Last Quarter Moon in Scorpio.

This Moon phase occurs at 22.17 UTC.

February 18 – Mercury Retrograde begins in Pisces.

During a retrograde period, it isn't the right time to move forward in any practical venture. Be prepared for misunderstandings and miscommunications to be prevalent.

February 23 - New Moon in Aquarius.

The Moon is on the same side of the Earth as the Sun and will not be visible in the night sky. This phase occurs at 15:32 UTC. This is an excellent time to view galaxies and stars as there is no moonlight to obscure your view of the universe.

FEBRUARY HOROSCOPE

FEBRUARY WEEK ONE

You have a right eye for detail, able to spot the potential or the pitfall in endeavors that you explore. You will navigate the path ahead and discover an opportunity which speaks to your analytical mind. It does relate to technology and communication. You transition towards an area which sees long term goals come into focus. It does take you towards developing dreams, and this creates a snowball effect which draws abundance into your world. You may feel that you are finding your feet in a new environment, but it does provide you with opportunities to plot a strategic course forward. This creates stable foundations, it does enable you to streamline your energy into areas which count the most. You may have been calculating the risk to reward ratio of getting involved with a new area. You are going to gain clarity, and the insight gained leads to a moment where you take a leap of faith and let your spirit guide you. It does prompt a significant turning point, and this can even lead to a breakthrough moment. It helps you navigate this uncertain time with a little more peace in your heart. You are someone who has a terrific ability to roll up your sleeves and turn your aspirations into reality. This marks a time where you begin to see clearly the path ahead, this creates a wellspring of new opportunities to help support growth. You are ready to progress your situation and bring something new into your world.

FEBRUARY WEEK TWO

The February 9th Supermoon flows a river of heightened potential into your sphere. Maintaining a steady course ahead is your best option. You can navigate uncertain times by keeping a balanced and patient outlook. More stability will gradually come into focus, it is a time which stretches your resources thin, but you have such a tenacious and resourceful spirit, you can glide your ship through dark waters and achieve a calmer outcome. Maintaining your focus on the goal ahead gives you a valuable post to aim for. You are a terrific family orientated person. You have instigated certain traditions which resonate warmly through your more full circle. You are someone with a lovely sense of joy, who can take care of others and bring fantastic outcomes to life. Good things are coming into your life. It may even reconnect you with a friendship long forgotten. This brings you a golden time to socialize, and a meet up with another lets you open your eyes to a situation which draws abundance into your world. It is a welcome boost to your life.

Furthermore, a gathering is coming, which shines a light on social prospects. An enchanting chapter is arriving for you soon. You make a discovery which leads to a deeper understanding of someone who captures your interest. It does signify a closer bond emerging, which ultimately leads you towards a more meaningful situation. This leads to soul-stirring conversations, which enable you to see growth in your personal sector. It does shine a light on harmony and happiness.

FEBRUARY WEEK THREE

This is an essential time for you, which sees your influence grow. It does show a sense of recognition arriving to encourage you to keep forging ahead towards the realization of your larger goals. You are earning a sense of prestige in an area which offers room for growth. This enables your outcomes to be successful, you can reap the rewards for the dedication given. The cosmic environment encourages you to circulate more in your wider community. It highlights a chance encounter occurring in the chapter head, which turns out to be fortuitous indeed. It is a beautiful time to mingle and enjoy what life has to offer. Focusing more on your social environment does pay dividends with some engaging encounters. It all leads to a memorable season to enjoy. You can expect an impressive result from a creative undertaking you get involved in. As a result of this venture, you discover further options to grow your talents. It could lead to a critical phase which sees you explore new possibilities. You are ready to shine in a new role, expanding your horizons is likely to be active and leads to beneficial outcomes. This is an exceptional time to plot a course which enables growth in your career sector. Under the influence of your careful planning, you can light a brilliant path towards success.

All in all, you make the most of this exciting phase. This is a favorable time to reap the wards of the magic in your life. You can expect more social invitations, and spending time with your tribe leads to fantastic brainstorming and sharing of thoughts and ideas. It is a time which heightens your creativity, and this gives you a real boost into a new level of potential. Pay attention to ideas which spark to life, they offer real gems.

FEBRUARY WEEK FOUR

You soon discover that you are not making enough time for yourself. While you may have obligations and commitments to oversee, it essential to nurture your own creative talents and forge a path which allows you to adequately seek the self-expression you crave. This self-nurturing is not selfish, it is imperative and does draw well-being into your world. Your life will brim with exciting outcomes soon. Opportunities arrive to tempt you out to an event or two. It does keep you busy and heightens your social aspect. There is a chance to update your skills and refine your talents with a refreshing course or learning path. There are opportunities to devote to creative projects, and having your unique stamp on an innovative venture leads to success. This is a superb time to open your eyes to the opportunities seeking to emerge in your life. These possibilities are helping to shape the path where you can enjoy the fruits of your labor. It does give you a reason to celebrate, and a positive outcome lights a route which offers growth and progression. You can advance your situation by being adaptable and flexible. Once your curiosity is sparked, you follow the leads which take you towards a path of growth and self-expression. Your situation is currently evolving, a shift forward is taking place.

MARCH ASTROLOGY

March 2 – First Quarter Moon in Gemini.

This Moon phase occurs at 19.57 UTC.

March 9 - Full Moon in Virgo, Supermoon.

This full Moon phase occurs at 17:48 UTC. This full moon is known as the Full Worm Moon because this was the time of year when the ground would soften, and earthworms would reappear. This full moon is also known as the Full Crow Moon, the Full Crust Moon, the Full Sap Moon, and the Lenten Moon. This is also the last of four super-moons for 2020. The Moon will be closer to the Earth and will look slightly larger and brighter than usual.

March 9 - Mercury Retrograde ends in Aquarius.

You can now move forward with any delayed plans that you have been putting off due to the Mercury Retrograde phase. Relationships should soon improve as miscommunications are overcome

March 16 – Last Quarter Moon in Sagittarius.

This Moon phase occurs at 9.34 UTC. –

March 20 - March Equinox.

The March equinox takes place at 3:50 UTC. The Sun be shining on the equator, and there will be equal amounts of day and night throughout the world. This is the first day of spring (vernal equinox) in the Northern Hemisphere.

March 24 - New Moon in Aries.

The Moon is on the same side of the Earth as the Sun and will not be visible in the night sky. This phase occurs at 9:28 UTC. This is an excellent time to observe galaxies and stars because there is no moonlight to interfere.

March 24 - Mercury at most substantial Western Elongation.

The planet Mercury reaches its most substantial western elongation of 27.8 degrees from the Sun.

March 24 - Venus at most substantial Eastern Elongation.

The planet Venus reaches its most substantial Eastern elongation of 46.1 degrees from the Sun.

MARCH HOROSCOPE

MARCH WEEK ONE

You may find yourself sifting through an emotionally tricky situation. Noticing patterns will help you connect with any blockages that could be holding you back. The insights you discover could lead to significant transformation, it does bring you to a chapter where you deal with unfinished business, you process past baggage, and transition to a brighter phase of potential. It's a beautiful time to create space for you. You are going for a total recalibration, this can turn your life upside down, but it also offers you a plethora of new options to explore. While you are in an air of intensity, you can dive deeply into uncharted waters which let you settle on an original path of abundance. It might take time before you indeed spread your wings in this different environment. It does see you healing blockages as you deal with heavy emotions. The universe is going to give you the green light to expand your life in beautiful ways. You can expect new information to yield innovative ideas which capture your interest. You may discover a colleague or kindred spirit wants to team up and test the collaborative synergy possible between you both. Ultimately, the more you invest in following your heart, the more stabilizing your energy becomes.

MARCH WEEK TWO

You may soon feel prompted towards healing areas which have limited progress in the past. It is a fruitful time to engage in modalities which nourish your soul. A strong focus on self-development does create a wonderfully reflective environment, you create space to release old patterns and regain your true potential. This initiates an active chapter of strengthening your core abilities. You can expect more lightness and levity to return to your life in the following section. It is a beautiful phase which initiates strong social growth and gives you the chance to spread your wings and mingle with kindred spirits. As you explore developing new collaborations, you share lively thoughts with others who understand you on a deeper level. It does give you a welcome opportunity to share your insightful opinions with eloquence. More opportunities are coming to socialize in your wider community. It is an exceptionally potent time for making new friends, mingling with others, and launching yourself in a new phase of potential. It all culminates in a highly active period which connects you to new friends and people. The opportunity to increase your inner circle is an invitation to broaden horizons.

Furthermore, opportunities are arriving for you soon, which support your higher goals. This will be an outlet for your restless energy, something you can focus on, which is in alignment with your current needs. It is a potent time to take action toward learning a new area. The crystallization of your awareness will enable you to spot an area worth exploring soon. This leads to a stabilizing time, which draws balance into your life. You are to be the recipient of positive news soon. A welcome surprise lands in your lap, this offer does entice you towards a new area of interest.

MARCH WEEK THREE

You are going through a time which may feel unsettling. A restless vibration is a current theme in your life, while this can feel disconcerting, you should be mindful that it is gently shifting your focus towards a more profound level of awareness. Ultimately, it is a path which is gently guiding you towards spiritual growth and represents a more solid phase of self-development occurring for you. You have handled some difficult situations which have given you a sense of growth and tenacity. The skills you have learned do enable you to progress further on your journey. You have hidden strength within you, which can be expressed in a fashion that takes you towards a different chapter of self-discovery. You are creating a surge of new opportunities by what has gone before.

Additionally, a new chapter is opening for you soon. It does lead to opportunities to grow your talents. You may find it challenging to move out of your comfort zone, remember, you are supported, guided, and nurtured by divine energy. You will receive signs through coincidences and serendipity, this helps give you feedback that you are headed in the right direction. The pace is set to heat up in your life, this relates to opportunities to socialize, and taking in community events which capture your interest. Your trajectory is leading towards advancement and growth. It does lead to a productive phase which puts a spotlight on your career and long-term goals. If in doubt, reach out to a mentor or other experienced person for advice. An opportunity arriving which aligns favorably with your future aspirations. It does set a strong focus on growth, while the workload could be demanding, it does lead to an expansion of growth. Sharing this with others is an excellent opportunity to collaborate and share the load.

MARCH WEEK FOUR

This week illuminates an enticing path ahead which puts the focus on good fortune and joint ventures. Collaboration is likely, it does bring your life a welcome bonus, it has you thinking about long-term potential. It sets the stage for adventures which inspire your mind. Long dormant emotions may arise as it does spark your interest as it captures your attention. This kicks off a phase linked to heightened confidence and well-being. You have done a great deal of work to transform your life. As your identity evolves, you are really coming into your own sense of confidence. You have a unique ability to harmonize the energy of others near you, this does see strong foundations being built with your closest ties. There is nothing you can't conquer if you set your mind to it. You are someone who has a creative and unique ability to breathe new life into your goals. This makes you both adaptable and innovative, you can test your ideas with new age technology and create a following. You could be a significant influencer of others, and as your trailblazing ideas gain traction with a broader audience, this does see your potential evolving to a new level.

APRIL ASTROLOGY

April 1 – First Quarter Moon in Cancer.

This Moon phase occurs at 10.21 UTC.

April 8 - Full Moon in Libra, Supermoon.

The Moon is on the opposite side of the Earth as the Sun and will be completely illuminated. This moon phase occurs at 2:35 UTC. This full moon is known as Full Pink Moon because it marked an appearance of the first spring flowers. This full moon has also been identified as the Sprouting Grass Moon, the Growing Moon, and the Egg Moon. Many coastal areas call it Full Fish Moon because this was the time the fish swam upriver to breed.

April 14 – Last Quarter Moon in Capricorn.

This Moon phase occurs at 22.56 UTC.

April 22, 23 - Lyrids Meteor Shower.

The Lyrids meteor shower runs each year from April 16-25. This meteor shower peaks on the night of the 22nd and the morning of the 23rd. These meteors sometimes produce blazing dust trails that last for several seconds.

April 23 - New Moon in Taurus.

The New Moon is on the same side of the Earth as the Sun and will not be visible in the night sky. This moon phase occurs at 2:26 UTC. This is an excellent time to observe galaxies and stars because there is no moonlight visible.

April 30 – First Quarter Moon in Leo.

This Moon phase occurs at 20.38 UTC.

APRIL HOROSCOPE

APRIL WEEK ONE

You are likely to get involved in a local venture soon. It does enable you to connect with some locals, and even a few unfamiliar faces soon become known to you. It does lead to a lively time where you can expand your social circle and take in a community event which captures your interest. It is a very grounded time where you draw lovely stability into your home life. There is a lot of new energy arriving in your life soon. This could lead to you having to make some adjustments as you are undergoing a process of change and transformation. If you feel tested by the events on the horizon, remember it does enable you to create space for a new chapter of potential. It does create a shift which is more adventurous and exciting. Surprise news soon arrives to tempt you out and about. This week emanates new potential coming in your world. This could see swift progress occurring as you transition to a fresh start. It leads to a breakthrough where you can release any outworn energy which has been causing doubt or confusion in your mind. It is a symbol which suggests that you are ready to enter a new area of growth and learning, expect a sign soon which sparks new ideas to life. This opportunity is specifically meant for you. It does open doors and puts a spotlight on friendly interactions, which see you getting involved in a local venture. You may find yourself networking with some unfamiliar faces, but it does plant the seeds for the birth of a creative project. It does bring growth on your doorstep, and your skills and talents add a certain finesse to this venture, which creates incredible potential.

APRIL WEEK TWO

If life has thrown you a curve ball recently, you can discover the way to bring harmony back. You have been going through a time of healing, closure, and release. As you transverse the path ahead, you head to a happier chapter. It does lift the stress and heaviness, which may have been draining your energy. Necessary changes are coming, which does draw lighter opportunities into your life. A weight lifts off your shoulders. You have made the correct choice for your situation. Although there have been difficulties surrounding you, you stood firm and made a stance for what you believed in. Your sense of authenticity and determination will hold you in good stead. Your emotional resilience is rising through the hurdles you overcome, soul-searching creates a healing environment. You are drawing resilience and courage into your world to create change and refresh the potential possible. It does illustrate the right conditions for you to engage in positive activities which boost your spirit. As you continue to move your energy towards developing your life by your core values, you do contemplate options which offer substantial avenues of personal development and growth. While this is a chapter which comes with some emotional intensity, you can overcome the nerves and release doubt as you can deal succinctly with issues that arise. There is a positive environment arriving soon. A shift is coming, which broadens your thinking and leaves you hungry to expand your horizons. The restlessness you currently are feeling is a call to step out of your usual routine and create space to revamp your life in the most revolutionary way. It does harness creative aspects which have a healing influence on your spirit. Looking at your options will bring an enticing area to light.

APRIL WEEK THREE

This is a reflective time, it does coax you to create space to resolve any problem areas which could be tugging at your emotional awareness. You make a longer and more therapeutic trip towards healing your spirit, it is an exceptional time to focus on your own personal goals and development. As you think about your resilience, you see that you have an innate ability to bounce back after setbacks. You are creating a shift which allows your energy to feel rested, it gets you excited about life in general and ready to face all that comes your way. You are making the right waves which allow you to sail forth into a new area of potential. This draws abundance and happiness into your world, it does help you focus on the blessings and release the baggage. You have a unique quality of being able to expand areas that you touch with your heart. This creates a ripple effect which draws people into your world. Support in your more extensive community being of benefit during this time. You have much to look forward to, there is a whole new layer of life to be revealed soon. It does make you aware of exciting possibilities, and it brings to the table new options which give you a strong sense of direction. It enables you to feel clear about creating space to bless your life with revolution. Your life has been marked by many contrasts, but you also can celebrate the highs. There will be a strong emphasis on renewing your energy and discovering a sense of purpose which inspires your mind. This encompasses drawing in new areas which offer room for progression. It does allow you to change your current pace and break free of limitations which have held back progress. It gives you a completely new mindset as you open your heart to the opportunities on your doorstep.

APRIL WEEK FOUR

You have come through an extensive phase of growing your spirit, it does bring a sense of healing into your world. Focusing on improving your situation does see progress occurring in home and family matters. This advancement is suitable for your spirit, it takes you towards growth, and gives you a clear idea of what projects you want to set in motion next. You are positioning yourself to advance your situation. Paying attention to your goals does play a crucial part in making that commitment to achieve a successful result. You are ready to take on more responsibilities, and learning is at the crux of a fascinating chapter ahead for you. One of your friends may also be instrumental in helping you accomplish your goals. Cover all your bases, leave no stone unturned. There will be surprise news ahead, which brings you to an exciting chapter. This rules an emotional aspect, and it does offer you room to follow your dreams. As a potential shimmer on the outskirts of your awareness, you can obtain a more accurate picture by spending a quiet moment in reflection. It helps you see larger patterns which are guiding your progress. You won't have to wait long to see new potential flowing into your world. It does set the stage for an impressive pace and provide you with an original source of inspiration. So many options are within your reach, spend time contemplating the path ahead so you can get a better understanding of the finer points of each area before embarking on your next journey.

MAY ASTROLOGY

May 6, 7 - Eta Aquarids Meteor Shower.

The Eta Aquarids meteor shower runs annually from April 19 to May 28. It peaks this year on the night of May 6 and the morning of May 7.

May 7 - Full Moon in Scorpio, Supermoon.

The Moon is on the opposite side of the Earth as the Sun, and its face will be fully illuminated. This phase occurs at 10:45 UTC. The May full moon is known as the Full Flower Moon because this was the time of year when spring flowers are in abundance. This full moon is also known as the Full Corn Planting Moon and the Milk Moon. This is also the last of four supermoons for 2020. The Moon will be at its closest approach to the Earth and looks slightly larger and brighter.

May 14 – Last Quarter Moon in Aquarius.

This Moon phase occurs at 14.03 UTC.

May 22 - New Moon in Taurus.

The Moon will be located on the same side of the Earth as the Sun and won't be seen in the night sky. This phase occurs at 17:39 UTC. The new moon phase is a brilliant time to observe galaxies and stars because there is no moonlight visible.

May 30 – First Quarter Moon in Virgo.

This Moon phase occurs at 3.30 UTC.

MAY HOROSCOPE

MAY WEEK ONE

This is an energizing time, the May 7th Supermoon leaves you feeling especially uplifted. An opportunity puts a pep in your step soon. It does feel exciting to be inspired by life. As you nail a new area to explore, it does draw excellent possibilities into your world. You may even be surprised by what is revealed over the following chapter. Your life is bubbling with all the new options ready to come to the surface. A special offer arriving for you soon. This is a time which propels you forward towards a more social aspect. It does culminate in invitations to mingle, there is a celebratory air which draws abundance into your world. A surprise is coming, and this leads to a chapter of adventure and excitement. It is a time which brings fun into your world, and there are days where you appreciate the blessings which inspire you to expand your life and grow your potential. You are thoughtful and kind. You will continue to inspire as you create positive impacts which reflect your light on others. There is a sense of creativity weaving through your life, you may feel guided to express yourself artistically, and create something unique and special. You have a magic touch and ample talents to share.

MAY WEEK TWO

You have unique abilities which surface unexpectedly and help you discover your more profound talents. You may have a yearning to expand your life, yet be unsure of which direction to head towards. Clarity is coming, and this does call your spirit most wonderfully. It does have you looking for a new avenue to develop, one which supports your life and nurtures your soul. This is a critical time to expand your options. It does provide you with avenues of growth which are hard to ignore. As you are tempted to create space for something special in your life, you cross the path of an opportunity which speaks to your heart. This does make it easy to move out of your usual routine and embrace new-found confidence. This relates to broadening your perception of what is possible in your life. It's an emotional awareness which expands your sense of well-being and does lead to personal growth. As you take in a vista of potential, you discover a path which eclipses that which has gone before. It does capture your inspiration and fills your mind with fresh ideas and excitement about the future. You are doing good work at uncovering opportunities which offer you real gems of potential. Filling your treasure chest with new options helps you discover a role which is perfect for your life. Something is going to be on offer for you which offers you room to dive into an area worth exploring. Understanding your calling will help you discover your destiny. Negotiations ahead which offer you a free chapter of advancement. You are likely to find yourself in the right environment to seal a deal which brings good fortune into your situation. This does relate to your career potential, there are indications that a change is in the air for you. You are ready to shine, and this inner confidence is going to hold you in good stead with any changes you decide to make.

MAY WEEK THREE

You should watch for fantastic news as something is ready to cross your path and complement your life as a nice bonus. It does have you smiling and brings on an enchanting avenue. This is a whole chapter to devote your energy towards personal growth. It does see some significant changes, which trigger a phase of advancement. The actions you take are instrumental in allowing this potential to unfold.

All in all, it makes this a significant chapter for you. There is a positive surprise emerging in your life soon. There is a more prominent theme of helping those in need, which is likely to provide your experience with a sense of purpose. You are making a journey towards an area which inspires your heart, it does have you spending time with people who draw meaning to your spirit. These occurrences are not just happenstance, it does introduce you to a new area which is meant specifically for you. There is an emphasis on expanding your social circle, it is wise to take advantage of the opportunities which arrive to tempt you out in your broader community. It does see you being in your element and brings joy and fun into your surroundings. Additionally, there are other benefits to be had by mingling and networking. It does offer you a sense of valuable well-being and brings a boost to your morale.

Luck and good fortune are available in your life, sometimes it can be challenging to spot the potential, gathering your resources and creating space for a meditative practice does work magic in the realm of getting in touch with your emotional awareness. Tapping into your intuition does broaden your life in a myriad of ways, it allows you to discover growth which can feel quite exciting, it also helps you pinpoint potential explicitly meant for you.

MAY WEEK FOUR

The past is a richly textured with emotional awareness, fond memories combine with a weaving path of growth and advancement. You currently are creating space to expand your life in a way which is aligned with your higher purpose. Discovering a path which speaks to the passion you have within your soul does take you towards your dreams. This advancement is an exciting environment from which to tap into your intuitive abilities. An open heart and a curious mind is your ticket to happiness. You emanate a positive approach which draws opportunities into your sphere. You can make headway on your goals, and as your ideas blossom in fertile ground, you do discover an area worth exploring. Spending time on achieving goals does let you rejuvenate your spirit and refuel your tanks of inspiration. If you have a felt worn thin by the demands of your life, things are set to change. You can connect with your intuition and discover a little worn path which offers room for growth. You may find soon that this area leads towards a chapter which is curious and insightful. It does surprise you with hidden gems of wisdom along the way. It pushes you to transform your life and broaden your perception of what is available in your situation. A breakthrough moment unleashes a welcome surprise.

Consequently, you can look forward to a happier chapter soon. You are ready to incorporate the lessons learned into a new section of potential. As you head towards brighter avenues, you upgrade your life and focus on building foundations which take you toward the fulfillment of goals. It is a great time where you can open your heart to expanding horizons while releasing areas which no longer hold your spirit. Your emotional resilience carries you through towards your dreams.

JUNE ASTROLOGY

June 4 - Mercury at Greatest Eastern Elongation.

The planet Mercury reaches greatest eastern elongation of 23.6 degrees from the Sun.

June 5 - Full Moon in Sagittarius.

The Full Moon is on the opposite side of the Earth as the Sun, and its face will be completely illuminated. This moon phase occurs at 19:12 UTC. This full moon is known as Full Strawberry Moon because it is the peak of the strawberry harvesting season. The June Full Moon has also been identified as the Full Rose Moon and the Full Honey Moon.

June 5 – Penumbral Lunar Eclipse.

This Moon eclipse occurs when the Moon passes through the Earth's partial shadow or penumbra. During this type of eclipse, the Moon will darken slightly but not completely disappear. This lunar eclipse will be visible throughout most of Europe, Africa, Asia, and Australia.

June 10 - Jupiter at Opposition.

The planet Jupiter will be at its nearest approach to Earth, and its planet face will be illuminated entirely by the Sun.

June 13 – Last Quarter Moon in Pisces.

This Moon phase occurs at 6.24 UTC.

June 17 – Mercury Retrograde begins in Cancer.

During a retrograde period, it isn't the right time to move forward in any practical venture. Be prepared for misunderstandings and miscommunications to be prevalent.

June 21 - June Solstice.

The June solstice occurs at 21:44 UTC. The North Pole will be tilted toward the Sun, which, having reached its northernmost position in the sky will be over the Tropic of Cancer at 23.44 degrees north latitude. This heralds the first day of summer (summer solstice) in the Northern Hemisphere, and is considered one of the most critical times of the year for many traditional cultures. It is the first day of winter (winter solstice) for the Southern Hemisphere.

June 21 - New Moon in Cancer.

The Moon is on the same side of the Earth as the Sun and will not be visible in the night sky. This moon phase occurs at 6:41 UTC. This is an excellent time to observe galaxies and stars because there is little moonlight to obstruct your view.

June 21 – Annual Solar Eclipse.

An annular solar eclipse occurs when the Moon is too far away from the Earth to completely cover the Sun. This results in a ring of light around the darkened Moon. The Sun's corona is not visible during an annular eclipse. The path of this solar eclipse begins in central Africa and travel through Saudi Arabia, northern India, and southern China before ending in the Pacific Ocean. A partial solar eclipse occurs throughout most of eastern Africa, the Middle East, and South Asia.

June 28 – First Quarter Moon in Libra.

This Moon phase occurs at 8.16 UTC.

JUNE HOROSCOPE

JUNE WEEK ONE

This week suggests the completion of a journey, a project or process you have been working on reaches its final conclusion. You can create space to honor this area, it may have felt like quite a journey to reach the pinnacle. It also allows you to begin the process of conceptualizing, what's next for you. Changes in the air, a shift is coming, which sees you embark on a new journey soon.

This reveals some exciting changes ahead for you. You may be feeling in a bit of a tailspin when a flurry of activity arrives to shake up your life. It does denote a time of adventure, which tempts you out in the broader community. This whirlwind of opportunity is part of a more prominent theme of opening your path and creating waves of new potential. You see that there are many options available to you. It does see more activity ahead for you, which creates a bustling hive of potential. It leads to a social chapter, and while you may find yourself navigating new environments, you can embrace meeting interesting characters, some of whom are likely to become firm friends. This expansion of your inner circle may even lead to a re-connection of an old friend. It is a time which brings long-awaited news. Some essential differences which weave through your life over the next chapter. It does bring more security as you enjoy life, you discover a shift towards a more social environment which draws abundance and well-being to your world. Your visionary aspect is on the rise, fueling a more prominent theme of adventure. It may even take you to a moment where you are willing to take a leap of faith and fly.

JUNE WEEK TWO

The planet Jupiter reaches its closest approach to the earth this week. It will be at its brightest, and this illuminates a new direction. Jupiters influence is one of luck, expansion, and good fortune. You peel back a chapter which inspires your mind. This sparks a new level of potential, which gets you stimulated about life. You head towards a situation which takes you out of your comfort zone, yet it encourages your mind and aligns favorably with your heart's desires. This becomes an important theme where you feel able to reach for your goals. It does shift you towards an abundant chapter of personal growth. As you draw fresh blessings into your surroundings, you drive a chapter forward, which is expansive, it shifts a more significant tide of abundance into your life. You are going through a section of considerable growth around your personal life. As you understand this influence better, it takes you towards developing ideas which head towards your dreams. It does suggest having a plan in place begins this chapter of rejuvenation. It is a fruitful season to embrace a new flow of energy. A quickening of pace does see an uptick of potential gain entry into your surroundings. This creates a cycle of growth, it is an influence which draws abundance, it does place a focus on obtaining a hard-won victory. This brings a significant turning point, it lets you focus on achieving a goal, which is lofty and inspiring.

JUNE WEEK THREE

The June 21st Solstice reveals a time which enables you to dig deep, bring up the old baggage to send packing out of your life. It is a beautiful time to pause and reflect on your goals. There may be an area which has been limiting your potential. If so, you can shake up this environment by broadening your options. A flexible and open approach does draw a blessing into your world. A lot of activity arrives at once, and as you sift through the options, you discover a path which is ripe for the taking. You enter a cycle of healing, and this enables you to create space to release an area which has held you back too long. As you make the necessary adjustments, you discover there is a lot of goodness to be found by focusing your energy forward. It begins a chapter which is generous and heartwarming. You touch down on a new area which inspires your mind and creates the type of advancement you have been seeking. You are in a cycle of growth and change. While it can bring a sense of unsettlement, which is disconcerting, it also unleashes a fresh flow of potential into your world. You can unmask a new chapter which reveals significant blessings arriving to support a journey of growth. Some of these changes may make you feel vulnerable. As you head out of your comfort zone, take time to rebalance your energy, and this will create a stable foundation.

JUNE WEEK FOUR

Mercury Retrograde sees that you may be facing difficulties head on this week. There may be a complicated situation causing anxiety and mental angst. It is a call to consider your options, perhaps something needs to be resolved for you to be ready to embrace a new chapter of potential. It does suggest clarity is arriving, which will give you the insight needed to resolve an issue which has been causing you consternation recently. This week relates to gaining insight into a difficult situation which has been on your mind lately. There is a person in your life that you have been conflicting with, and this has led to emotional stress. Taking time to unlock the puzzle, you can achieve a better outcome by utilizing the power of your intuition. It also is a time which encourages you to be creative and make a bold decision. You may have been juggling various demands on your time, work, and home commitments have taken a toll on your free time. You now have an opportunity to boost your emotional resources and create time to ground your spirit. This draws harmony into your life and does lead to more stability ahead. Life will calm down to a more manageable pace soon.

JULY ASTROLOGY

July 5 - Full Moon in Capricorn.

The July Full Moon is located on the opposite side of the Earth as the Sun and will be fully illuminated. This phase occurs at 4:44 UTC. This full moon is known as Full Buck Moon because the male buck deer start to grow new antlers. This full moon is also known as the Full Thunder Moon and the Full Hay Moon.

July 5 – Penumbral Lunar Eclipse.

This Moon eclipse occurs when the Moon passes through the Earth's partial shadow or penumbra. During this type of eclipse, the Moon will darken slightly but not completely disappear. This lunar eclipse will be visible throughout most of Europe, Africa, Asia, and Australia.

July 12 – Last Quarter Moon in Aries.

This Moon phase occurs at 23.29 UTC.

July 12 - Mercury Retrograde ends in Cancer.

You can now move forward with any delayed plans that you have been putting off due to the Mercury Retrograde phase. Relationships should soon improve as communication improves.

July 14 - Jupiter at Opposition.

The Giant planet Jupiter will be at its nearest approach to Earth and will be at it's brightest.

July 20 - New Moon in Cancer.

The July New Moon is located on the same side of the Earth as the Sun and won't be visible in the night sky. This moon phase occurs at 17:33 UTC. This is an excellent time to observe galaxies and stars because there is no moonlight visible.

July 20 - Saturn at Opposition.

The beautiful ringed planet Saturn will be at its nearest approach to Earth and will be illuminated by the Sun.

July 22 - Mercury at Greatest Western Elongation.

The planet Mercury reaches greatest western elongation of 20.1 degrees from the Sun.

July 27 – First Quarter Moon in Scorpio.

This Moon phase occurs at 12.32 UTC.

July 28, 29 - Delta Aquarids Meteor Shower.

The Delta Aquarids meteor shower peaks on the night of July 28 and morning of July 29. The first quarter moon may block many of the fainter meteors this year. You should still be able to view the brighter ones. Best viewing will be at a dark vista after midnight. Meteors radiate from the constellation Aquarius but can appear anywhere in the sky.

JULY HOROSCOPE

JULY WEEK ONE

The full moon this week connects you to your intuition and higher wisdom. This week is strongly correlated with the moon, which is a full moon tonight. There is a serendipitous event which adds additional weight to her presence in your life. You are asked to go within and create space to reflect on that which needs to be healed to create peace. She; the moon helps to guide your path correctly. This week connects you to light energy, it speaks of dreams and goals manifesting into reality. There is a beautiful element of abundance likely to arrive, which boosts your spirit and has you drinking from a well of abundance. You can set your sights on lofty goals and achieve excellent outcomes during this fortuitous chapter. This is the time in which you can create space to nurture your life and focus on developing a path which draws happiness. It's an ideal opportunity to circulate in the wider community and become open to personal growth. It does lead to improved family relationships and suggests a generous and heartwarming time is arriving soon. This is a time of beginning a new emotional journey. It is the beginning of a cycle that draws more abundance and well-being into your world. It is connected to the development of a bond which brings joy to your life. This can have a profoundly positive effect on your situation. It does highlight expanding your horizons and creating space for someone new to arrive.

JULY WEEK TWO

Mercury Retrograde ends on the 12th of July, and this sees you successfully emerge from a cocoon where you have sheltered your creativity recently. This week relates to finding your feet again after an unsettling time. You may be feeling restless, and at loggerheads with the direction, you are heading. It is always a great idea to stay open to new information and options, a change is coming, which enables you to climb a path of growth. It leads to a fantastic aspect which gives your situation and overhaul and lets you enjoy quality time doing something which inspires your mind. If you have felt sensitive recently, it is because of a shift in your emotional awareness, this intensity does get your attention, and it is best to take a break and create space to refresh your perspective. Maybe there is an alternative route which enables growth to occur more smoothly. Your emotional resilience is on the rise, as well as your creativity and problem-solving abilities. You are in a regular cycle of healing, growth, and good fortune. This elevates your potential, it takes you towards a chapter filled with hope and inspiration. A venture you begin during this time is likely to be successful and draw abundance into your world. Going after your dreams helps you live your life with passion and joy. A welcome surprise arriving in your inbox soon.

JULY WEEK THREE

You enter a chapter which heightens your creativity and coaxes you to expand your life by learning new areas. This draws opportunity into your environment, experimenting with different avenues brings you a project you can develop. It is a beautiful time of combining ideas with others and tapping into fresh inspiration, which shines a brilliant light on the potential possible. It does lead to an original and adventurous path forward. It's going to be a beautiful chapter for you, it does see you making new friends and being more social. Having some extra invitations arrive gives you a reason to celebrate. Your confidence is rising, and being open to new environments does tap into an adventurous time ahead. You can harness a sense of self-expression and creativity to mark the occasion with a unique flair and style. This is a great time to draw abundance on a deeper level. It does bring you to a more social aspect and has you building memories which count. An invitation arrives, which inspires your mind, it leads to an enchanting adventure. This draws excitement and joy into your world, it is a time which brings new surprises into your world, and this becomes the icing on the cake for you.

JULY WEEK FOUR

There is a growing emphasis on creating abundance in your life, you may be planning for something important, or have something big in mind. It is serious business, you are ready to focus on obtaining a successful result. This does see progress being made, and as you soon get positive feedback for the work undertaken, you are inspired to keep your nose to the grindstone and see this to completion. It does take you towards a happier chapter, one which nurtures your passions and gives you the drive to move into a new area. It is a thoughtful time which focuses on creative aspects, it does help you take your talents to the next level. The power of this chapter cannot be underestimated, as it does reveal a substantial phase of growth and self-development. Examining your higher goals sets the stage for future progress. This is a time of forwarding motion, there is activity coming, which sees you shift towards a more active phase. It does turn up the potential in your life and blesses your world with robust possibilities. It is a time of heightened courage and confidence, enabling you to boldly step out of your comfort zone. Furthermore, you may discover a sense of rejuvenation revives your personal life.

AUGUST ASTROLOGY

August 3 - Full Moon in Aquarius.

The August Full Moon is located on the opposite side of the Earth as the Sun and will be fully illuminated. This phase occurs at 15:59 UTC. The August full moon is known as the Full Sturgeon Moon because sturgeon fish of the Great Lakes and other major lakes were quickly caught during this time. This full moon has also been known as the Green Corn Moon and the Grain Moon.

August 11 – Last Quarter Moon in Taurus.

This Moon phase occurs at 16.45 UTC.

August 12, 13 - Perseids Meteor Shower.

The Perseids meteor shower runs each year from July 17 to August 24. It peaks this year on the night of August 12 and the morning of August 13. The Perseids meteor shower is one of the best to view as the meteors are so bright and numerous. The best viewing is from a dark vista after midnight.

August 13 - Venus at Greatest Western Elongation.

The planet Venus reaches greatest western elongation of 45.8 degrees from the Sun.

August 19 - New Moon in Leo.

The Moon will be on the same side of the Earth as the Sun and will not be visible in the night sky. This moon phase occurs at 2:41 UTC. This is an excellent time to observe galaxies and stars because there is no moonlight to obstruct the view.

August 25 – First Quarter Moon in Scorpio.

This Moon phase occurs at 17.58 UTC.

AUGUST HOROSCOPE

AUGUST WEEK ONE

You glide through a chapter which offers you many benefits. A matter of great personal importance reaches a successful conclusion. As this comes to fruition, you appreciate the journey which has gone before. Any delays in progress are no longer an issue, you can begin to plot a course towards a long term goal. It is a brilliant time which brings a bountiful harvest into your world. This is a vital phase filled with growth orientated opportunities. You wrap up an area which may have felt tedious, as this project reaches a successful conclusion, it enables you to make a huge leap forward towards a new chapter of potential. It is a time where you can pursue your goals, life's circumstances propel you forwards, and this spotlights a happy and fortuitous section emerging in your world. It is a time where you can explore the possibilities and create a significant change forward in your evolution. It is a creative time which sees you craft base potential and molds it into something spectacular. This process of refinement enables you to spot the opportunity and positively transform your situation. There are many changes which resonate through your life, your intuition guides you correctly.

Something arrives for you out of the blue, it advances your potential and opens your eyes to a new area. This gives you a welcome change, it is a critical time to focus on an area which holds special significance to you. As you harmonize your life by focusing on that which brings you joy, you rework the potential possible and draw abundance into your world.

AUGUST WEEK TWO

You see an influx of information which arrives at your doorstep to surprise you with opportunities to make you smile. It does focus on developing a personal situation, you feel encouraged by the feelings of affection which surround this potential. It is a chapter where your confidence rises, and as you expand your horizons, you are happy and content with the progress you achieve. Your star is growing, you are gaining the attention of others, and this does lead to favorable changes in your situation. A creative undertaking is likely and offers you room to grow your talents. You increasingly find that your life is on an upswing, it does see you garner favor from someone who can boost your situation. It is a phase of opportunities and optimism which sees your life blossom. Your life is set to be more active soon, crucial new information arrives, which does offer you a chance to progress a goal you may have in mind. It does see you teaming up and collaborating with another, sharing your options opens a floodgate of new potential, it gives you possibilities to expand your horizons, and it draws a valuable sense of well-being into your life. Caring for yourself is an essential ingredient for your well-being at this time. It does give your spirit a powerful boost, and you are set to benefit from a more productive and happy chapter. Abundance is ready to make itself known, you can expand your horizons and discover a path which offers you a sense of rejuvenation.

AUGUST WEEK THREE

This is a fortuitous time for you. New opportunities arrive to tempt you out in your wider community. It does polarise your focus on drawing abundance into your situation. It is a chapter which gives gifts and luck, showing your willingness to be open to this potential does allow the floodgates to open and secures your bounty. These welcome surprises are your ticket to a fun time. Abundant gifts, luck, and good fortune are likely to be prominent in your life. Soon, it has you thinking broadly about the possibilities you can explore. It does give you a better deal and simply reminds you to expand your horizons and appreciate the abundance which seeks to emerge in your life. This beautiful aspect does help you bright space and release outworn areas which ultimately have held progress back. This is an abundant and magical phase for you. It does exert a secure flow of fortune into your life, and this draws abundance into your world. You are likely to be excited and pleasantly surprised by what occurs in the following phase. It blends perfectly with current goals, and it does add a beneficial aspect to your life, which lightens your surroundings. A lovely surprise is coming for you soon. There is a spontaneous factor that plays beautifully with this opportunity. It does have you feeling excited about the potential. It leads to active time, which brings you fantastic news and does reward you with excellent outcomes. You discover that your timing is perfect, and you connect to a situation which feels lucky.

AUGUST WEEK FOUR

Lovely surprises are coming which enable you to adjust to a new chapter, no longer feeling at loggerheads with moving forward, it offers you a sense of direction and the ability to progress your situation tangibly. While the past has a strong influence over you, you are ready to make strides in a new area. As you navigate this phase, you can continue to string think actively about your goals. There are lots of options to investigate, depending on your goals, you may discover an area which offers you a surprising prescription for well-being. It becomes an extension of your current situation, giving you a wonderful sense of accomplishment as you achieve an important win. Upgrading your life brings you to a chapter imbued with a powerful sense of creativity. Being present and keeping a lookout for an option which sees you star in a new role. It does lead to an abundant and magical time, which lights a compelling path forward. Happily, you are ready for these changes and can harness your adaptability and flexibility to power through any nerves you may have about moving out of your comfort zone. The air of manifestation runs through this phase.

SEPTEMBER ASTROLOGY

September 2 - Full Moon in Pisces.

The September full Moon is on the opposite side of the Earth as the Sun, and its face will be fully illuminated. This phase occurs at 5:22 UTC. This full moon is known as the Full Corn Moon because the corn is harvested around this time.

September 10 – Last Quarter Moon in Gemini.

This Moon phase occurs at 9.26 UTC.

September 11 - Neptune at Opposition.

The giant blue planet will be at its closest approach to Earth, and its face will be illuminated by the Sun.

September 17 - New Moon in Virgo.

The Moon is on the same side of the Earth as the Sun and will not be visible in the night sky. This phase occurs at 11:00 UTC. This is an excellent time to observe galaxies and stars because there is no moonlight visible.

September 22 - September Equinox.

The 2020 September equinox occurs at 13:31 UTC. The Sun shines directly on the equator, creating equal amounts of day and night throughout the world. This is also the first day of fall (autumnal equinox) in the northern hemisphere and is considered a significant zodiac event for many traditional cultures.

September 24 – First Quarter Moon in Capricorn.

This Moon phase occurs at 1.55 UTC.

SEPTEMBER HOROSCOPE

SEPTEMBER WEEK ONE

There may be some adjustments which cause growing pains. It does prompt you to deal with your situation with a fresh approach. You no longer follow old patterns, this ultimately leads to a happier chapter. You have grown into a strong and capable person. Your resilience and intelligence set you apart from your peers. You are going to reveal a journey which inspires you to expand your horizons. As you contemplate the options before you, you will discover a path which offers a bounty of opportunities. It does start jump start an active phase of growth for you. It is a time for clearing the air and obtaining clarity into a personal situation. You may feel you are reaching a crossroads, a situation requires decisive action. This brings you to a crucial turning point, it does have you exploring the possibilities and getting a better idea of where you are headed with someone of interest. There is an adventurous element which brings new potential into what may be flagging. You may have felt confused about a personal situation, there is something in the pipeline, which leads to a significant change of fortune in your life. This process takes time to unfold, but as it ramps up the potential in your world, it does have you seeing a positive influx of joy. This relates to developing a situation with someone special, it does bring a new layer of abundance into your life.

SEPTEMBER WEEK TWO

The planet Neptune is at its closest approach to Earth this week, it will be at its brightest. Neptune rules your house of dreams and healing. It is darkest before the dawn, blockages which limit your true potential can be lifted by broadening your perception of what is possible in your situation. Staying true to your inner guidance, and make choices, which are in alignment with your emotional awareness sees the difficulties which trouble your spirit lighten, breaking free of the areas which hold you back, does open the door to positive change. You may be feeling blocked and restricted, you can get to the bottom of these feelings by looking at what is holding you back. The past has gifted you with strength and fortitude, you can deepen your awareness, which enables you to overcome obstacles and reach for a path which is fulfilling and in alignment with your soul's purpose.

This week foretells of a change in direction for you. It is strongly connected with fortune, fate, and good luck. It takes you towards a decisive breakthrough, this substantially alters your perspective of what is possible in your situation. It does help guide you towards smoother waters. Staying open to a positive sign lets you spot a window of opportunity which opens and provide you with a beautiful path of growth. You can navigate through life's difficulties with a steady and secure approach. Your flexibility and tenacity enable considerable personal growth. Drawing new goals into your life leads to an uplifting time, which has a highly social aspect. New friends enter your life, and you do benefit from an influx of invitations which expand your horizons. It does see you connect with an inspirational character who has a great deal of wisdom to share.

SEPTEMBER WEEK THREE

Your communication skills are on the rise, this gives you more confidence to expand your social horizons. It enables you to break through limitations and even forge a new alliance soon. Speaking openly and authentically from the heart brings you closer to one who captures your interest. This does see a situation unfolding which offers room for growth. This person characterizes the positive energy of fire, this one is dynamic, active, and inspirational. This is a person who pursues goals and desires with innate confidence. This character has a unique style and likes to do things with a sense of pizzazz. Their flair for creating abundance and brightness is sure to dazzle and capture your awareness. It is a situation which provides you with a sense of happiness and joy. You can prepare to celebrate soon, it does see you spending time with others, and there is a happy element which offers a highly social aspect. Connecting with lively characters, you open the potential to build deeper bonds. It does lead to a time of happiness, a sense of joy flows into your life, which has a soothing effect on your spirit. It is the perfect boost which offers you opportunities in your personal life.

SEPTEMBER WEEK FOUR

The Equinox this week arrives to allow you the ability to harness the power of manifestation. This is a beautiful phase because it speaks of your own personal power and your ability to influence outcomes. This week speaks of a significant moment occurring, which sees something important come to fruition in your life. It does signify happiness and joy is on its way, you appreciate this bonus as it does mark a turning point of fortune in your world. This is a welcome boost which offers you room to grow your situation.

Additionally, you begin to see larger goals come into focus due to the changes ahead. There will be something new happening, which has you focused on improving your situation. It does have you negotiating a path which feels adventurous, it suggests a goal comes into focus, which makes all the difference for your situation. It is an active time where you can obtain clarification by doing research on this topic of interest. It does take on a life of its own, once you get the ball rolling. Unexpected news is coming which gives you an assignment, you can sink your teeth into. It does bring an amount of good fortune into your life, this puts a smile on your face as it heightens an aspect of creativity, which keeps you feeling focused and inspired. You are a free spirit and harness a sense of adventure during the changes ahead. It does bring something favorable to your table.

OCTOBER ASTROLOGY

October 1 - Full Moon in Aries.

The October full Moon is on the opposite side of the Earth as the Sun, and its face will be fully illuminated. This phase occurs at 21:05 UTC. This full moon is known as the Hunters Moon because at this time of year the leaves are falling, and the game is ready. This full moon is also known as the Travel Moon and the Blood Moon. This moon is also known as the Harvest Moon. The Harvest Moon is the full moon that occurs closest to the September equinox each year.

October 1 - Mercury at Greatest Eastern Elongation.

The planet Mercury reaches greatest eastern elongation of 25.8 degrees from the Sun.

October 7 - Draconids Meteor Shower.

The Draconids meteor shower runs annually from October 6-10 and peaks this year on the night of the 7[th.]

October 10 – Last Quarter Moon in Cancer.

This Moon phase occurs at 0.39 UTC.

October 13 – Mercury Retrograde begins in Scorpio.

During a retrograde period, it isn't the right time to move forward in any practical venture. Be prepared for misunderstandings and miscommunications to be more prevalent.

October 16 - New Moon in Libra.

The Moon will be on the same side of the Earth as the Sun and will not be seen in the night sky. This moon phase occurs at 19:31 UTC. This is an excellent time of the month to view galaxies and stars because there is no moonlight visible.

October 21, 22 - Orionids Meteor Shower.

The Orionids meteor shower runs yearly from October 2 to November 7. Orionids meteor shower peaks this year on the night of October 21 and the morning of October 22.

October 23 – First Quarter Moon in Capricorn.

This Moon phase occurs at 13.23 UTC.

October 31 - Full Moon, Blue Moon in Taurus.

The October full Blue Moon is on the opposite side of the Earth as the Sun, and its face will be fully illuminated. This phase occurs at 14:49 UTC. This is the second full moon in the same month, it is referred to as a blue moon.

October 31 - Uranus at Opposition.

The planet Uranus will be at its nearest approach to Earth, and its face will be illuminated by the Sun.

OCTOBER HOROSCOPE

OCTOBER WEEK ONE

This is an ideal time to craft new plans and explore a more full field of vision. As new options enter, you transition forward to a more industrious chapter. Your creativity is on the rise, an influx of potential arrives to tempt you towards growth. It does see the setting of goals, having an aspiring new path does plant the seeds, which in time grow into something significant for you. You enter an active phase of developing goals. An opportunity arrives to give you the green light, this allows you to move forward and start an area which is in alignment with your future goals. This becomes the foundation from which you grow your talents. The goals you set for yourself give you a clear path ahead and provide you with objective feedback. An uplifting time arrives to provide you with a welcome boost. It begins a chapter of new ideas, planting seeds of inspiration, you can plot a course towards future growth. Your ideas and thoughts combine to offer you the chance to advance your situation, your subconscious awareness is guiding this process, paying attention to your intuition is beneficial. You are ready to bring something new into your life, it is a time which enables you to go after an expansive vision. Taking proactive steps to improve your situation does draw the right type of potential in your world. Intuitive flashes guiding your progress forward. Furthermore, social invitations arrive to tempt you to try new activities.

OCTOBER WEEK TWO

Things begin to improve as a forward motion brings a sense of rejuvenation into your life. This quickly restores drained energy and does lead to improved well-being. Taking dedicated steps to tackle your dreams provides you with a focus which can sweep in significant changes, it points towards abundance as life becomes more energized. Exciting changes are coming, which kick off a chapter of inspiration and social engagement. A crew of fascinating characters who form part of your more comprehensive social connection becomes more prominent, these individuals weave through your life and bring a valuable sense of connection into your world. This stability becomes the basis from which you can expand your life and take in some adventurous horizons in the next chapter. Excitement features prominently in the section ahead. You are headed to a bright and lively time where your goals shine a path towards achieving something special. Advancement is lighting a route which offers you some fascinating areas to develop, even if there is a detour or two along the way, these side journeys are often the most rewarding.

OCTOBER WEEK THREE

You have a gift of an entrepreneurial nature, there is a breakthrough area which offers you room to grow your talents, it does bring your contributions to our wider audience, you discover that you enjoy this creative process, your input does put a unique stamp on the potential possible. Your horizons are broadening, as you spot an exciting area to focus on. An impressive offer may cross your path soon. There is a change arriving which is due to a heightening of creativity, this usher in ideas which pave the way towards a lively chapter. You thrive in a busy and active environment, and it shines a spotlight on social ties and does draw happiness into your world. Impressive results are achievable, broadening your perception, being willing to open your mind to new opportunities and environments to provide you with a valuable trajectory. There are some beautiful gems to be unearthed if you explore your more extensive world. You can revolutionize and rejuvenate your situation, and this creates space for a shift towards a happy chapter. Currently, you are at a crossroads, this suggests a cycle of change and growth is emerging. It does shift you towards a more joyful section and leads towards a path which shimmers with new potential.

OCTOBER WEEK FOUR

The rare Full Blue Moon this week says it is a time of abundance and magic. You enter the house of closure, it does signify essential changes occurring in your situation, while you are reaching a new chapter, you can look back at the past and be proud of how you have grown your wisdom. Something arrives by surprise, which dramatically opens a new doorway to tend you forward. An opportunity comes for you soon, if you have been feeling dissatisfied with the current environment, you will be excited at new energy to pour your energy into shortly. This becomes a cherished path which brings a personal goal to the forefront of your awareness. It does lead to a time which offers you plenty of wiggle room to bring your dreams to life. It is a fantastic time to nurture your spirit and heel areas which have impeded progress. Building the right foundations within your core, to provide you with strength and tenacity, this resilience becomes a powerhouse of potential, it enables you to transform your life from the inside out, and it does see you breakthrough limitations and shift towards a more positive aspect.

NOVEMBER ASTROLOGY

November 3 - Mercury Retrograde ends in Libra.

You can now move forward with any delayed plans that you have been putting off due to the Mercury Retrograde phase. Relationships should soon improve as miscommunications resolve.

November 4, 5 - Taurids Meteor Shower.

The Taurids meteor shower runs yearly from September 7 to December 10. It peaks this year on the night of November 4.

November 8 – Last Quarter Moon in Leo.

This Moon phase occurs at 13.46 UTC.

November 15 - New Moon in Scorpio.

The Moon is on the same side of the Earth as the Sun and will not be visible in the night sky. This phase occurs at 5:07 UTC. This is an excellent time to view galaxies and star clusters because there is no moonlight visible.

November 17, 18 - Leonids Meteor Shower.

The Leonids meteor shower runs yearly from November 6-30. The Leonids meteor shower peaks this year on the night of the 17th and morning of the 18th.

November 22 – First Quarter Moon in Pisces.

This Moon phase occurs at 4.45 UTC.

November 30 - Full Moon in Gemini.

The November full Moon is on the opposite side of the Earth as the Sun, and its face will be fully illuminated. This phase occurs at 9:30 UTC. This full moon is known as Full Beaver Moon as this was the time of year to set beaver traps before the swamps and rivers froze. It is also known as the Frosty Moon and the Hunter's Moon.

November 30 - Penumbral Lunar Eclipse

A penumbral lunar eclipse occurs when the Moon passes through the Earth's partial shadow or penumbra. During this type of eclipse, the Moon will darken but not completely eclipse. This Penumbral lunar eclipse will be visible throughout most of North America, the Pacific Ocean, and northeastern Asia.

NOVEMBER HOROSCOPE

NOVEMBER WEEK ONE

The Taurids meteor shower which peaks on November 4th illuminates recent information regarding an influence surrounding your life, which could be holding back progress. You are headed towards an essential chapter which rejuvenates your situation, it reinvents certain areas of your life and provides you with a valuable outlet for your talents. It is a beautiful time of setting goals and planning for future projects. As your mine lights up with fresh inspiration, you can realize that you are sitting on a goldmine of potential. A phase of advancement is unfurling in your life, big-picture plans begin to take shape, you have what it takes to see your goals to fruition and create success in the physical realm. It is a beautiful time of expanding your life and activating new potential, which is at the foundation of an active phase of growth for you. Your confidence is on the rise, you are headed towards an extensive stage, which is bold and adventurous. It does see you brewing up new ideas, mingling with others who have similar values and mindsets. It does lead to a crest which inspires and encourages positive change in your world.

NOVEMBER WEEK TWO

You are headed towards a chapter which marks a beautiful new beginning, there is a strong theme weaving through your life, which in essence reflects your ability to overcome hurdles, and maintain flexibility as you transition towards new levels of growth and learning. It is a time where you can reflect on these changes and appreciate the depth of understanding, which guides your process forward. A reward is coming, which helps you find a path that enables headway to occur. You can set aside doubt, releasing the fear of failure, and trust that you can make a new area shine with your unique gifts. Utilizing your talents takes you on a journey which offers objective feedback, it does flow towards the realization of dreams. You weed out areas which have been limiting progress, if you have found stuck, setting boundaries with areas which impede your potential does provide you with a beautiful shift forward. Not having to fight to swim upstream does enable you to focus on developing regions which hold the most exceptional promise. It is also healing and therapeutic, allowing you to nourish your spirit. It is a time of crafting new goals and taking advantage of the flow of inspiration, which helps you to embark on a journey which is adventurous and exciting. Barriers are dissolved, it is an expensive time where you can light the fire to new potential, and explore the broader world of possibility which seeks to tempt you towards growth and change. This is a chapter of further information, heighten communication, and life opportunities to discuss and share thoughts and ideas. It does put you in the mood to mingle, friends and associates reach out and touch base with you. Having this extra opportunity to socialize does heighten the sense of connection in your world and provide you with meaningful feelings of grounded joy.

NOVEMBER WEEK THREE

There is an area which has created a blockage, taking time to focus on healing the past does release outworn energy. This is an ideal time to focus on improving the past, a time of self-reflection gets the ball rolling, you create an essential space to honor the past, yet also to release areas which only limited progress. Analyzing these areas, you begin to see that they really do serve no higher purpose in your world. Learning to nourish your spirit with emotionally rewarding areas will bring you the highest return. Exciting changes of flow into your world and provide you with a sense of joy, this energy is buoyant and lively, it does lift your spirits, a turning point is reached, which sees old areas are released, and it gives you a feeling that you can finally move forward and begin a new vision. Drawing inspiration into your spirit is a crucial step to start the process of creating change. You can accomplish valuable healing through nurturing a sense of self-awareness, understanding what triggers you negatively will help you sidestep these areas and spotlight paths which allow you to deflect and move away from these issues before they take a negative hold on your spirit. A golden opportunity arriving, which triggers a lovely phase of excitement for you.

NOVEMBER WEEK FOUR

Opportunities are coming, which will widen your social circle, it allows you to engage more with your wider community, new friends arrive to support social growth and well-being. A surprising invitation arrives, which triggers the unique potential for you. You can connect with a broader audience, it does bring you a valuable sense of togetherness, spending time with kindred spirits. Provides you with feelings of joy and well-being. Even those you haven't met yet can impact your mood on a beneficial level. It does reshuffle the decks of potential as it ignites new opportunities for growth. This is a time where you can be open to bursts of inspiration, your creativity is on the rise, this reawakens long forgotten talents and provide you with ample opportunities to expand your skill set. It does lead to a broadening of horizons as you find valuable paths which bring you growth and give you a chance to shine. There is a venture on offer, it does relate to an area which is close to your heart, as you are excited and enthusiastic about the potential possible, you feel re-energized, it leads to an important chapter where you can shift your focus for words and begin a journey of growth and development. You can prepare to launch forward with a trajectory which is adventurous and inspiring.

DECEMBER ASTROLOGY

December 8 – Last Quarter Moon in Virgo.

This Moon phase occurs at 0.37 UTC.

December 13, 14,15 - Geminids Meteor Shower.

The Geminids meteor shower runs each year from December 7-17. The Geminids meteor showers peaks this year on the night of the 13th, 14th, and 15th. The nearly new moon this year will provide dark skies for an excellent show. Best viewing will be from a dim vista after midnight. Meteors will radiate from the constellation Gemini but can appear anywhere in the sky.

December 14 - New Moon in Sagittarius.

The Moon is on the same side of the Earth as the Sun and will not be visible in the night sky. This moon phase occurs at 16:17 UTC. This is an excellent time to view galaxies and stars because there is no moonlight visible.

December 21 – First Quarter Moon in Pisces.

This Moon phase occurs at 23.41 UTC.

December 21 - December Solstice.

The 2020 December solstice occurs at 10:02 UTC. The South Pole of the earth tilts toward the Sun, which, having reached its most southern place in the sky, is directly over the Tropic of Capricorn at 23.44 degrees south latitude. This December solstice also marks the first day of winter (winter solstice) in the Northern Hemisphere.

December 21 – Great Conjunction of Jupiter and Saturn.

A conjunction of Jupiter and Saturn will take place on December 21. This is known as the great conjunction as it is a rare celestial event. The last great conjunction occurred in the year 2000. The two bright planets will appear only 7 arc minutes of each other in the night sky. They will be so close that they will seem to make a bright double planet. Look to the west just after sunset for this impressive and rare planetary pair.

December 21, 22 - Ursids Meteor Shower.

The Ursids meteor shower occurs each year from December 17 - 25. This meteor event peaks this year on the night of the 21st and morning of the 22nd.

December 30 - Full Moon in Cancer.

The Moon is on the opposite side of the Earth as the Sun, and its face will be fully illuminated. This moon phase occurs at 03:28 UTC. This full moon is known as the Full Cold Moon because this is the time of year when the cold winters air arrives and nights become long and dark. This full moon is known as the Long Nights Moon and the Moon Before Yule.

DECEMBER HOROSCOPE

DECEMBER WEEK ONE

This is the time which focuses on developing a stable path forward. It does relate to getting the most out of your skills and talents, you can shine and achieve a stellar result. Taking pride in your work does Garver the interest of others who notice your diligence and dedication towards completing a top outcome. You are emotionally resilient, tenacious, and have a fantastic strength of character. This allows you to navigate hurdles, overcome barriers, and move past obstacles, the more you better your situation, the more you realize that the decisions you make are instrumental in creating positive change in your world. This is a valuable time which kicks off a new cycle of growth for you. You are ready to advance your goals, your vibrancy is radiating positive outcomes. You can take advantage of an offer which arrives to tempt you towards a new horizon. Being proactive and bold does lead to a bountiful cycle of fortuitous energy. Something you are focused on comes together nicely for you. This marks the beginning of a new chapter as a cherished personal goal reaching fruition. Your sense of self-expression and identity become bolder, and this is a wake-up call that your horizons are expanding. An influx of fresh ideas leads to clarity, and this fuels your potential.

DECEMBER WEEK TWO

You are balancing many demands on your time, it does deplete your energy, but also reward you with a growing sense of abundance. The work you do is creating space for something beautiful to enter your life. This does bring you towards a chapter of expanding your situation and transforming it into a beautiful phase of structured growth. You are transitioning to a branch which bears heightened opportunities for growth and stability. Creating more substance in your life does allow you to tackle big-picture dreams, your power of manifestation runs swiftly through this phase, it does take you towards action driven tasks, a productive chapter sets the stage for future growth. You are heading towards a section which lifts your spirits, news arrives soon, which brings you joy. It does give you an offer of valuable support from one who nourishes your courage. Lively discussions lead to productive dialogues, and new ideas are at the foundation of this beautiful phase. Planning for future goals. Does bring you a wonderful sense of inspiration and excitement.

DECEMBER WEEK THREE

This is a time which offers a chance to socialize and mingle. You can enjoy focusing on activities which enable you to unwind with a larger group of people. A celebration or highly significant event is likely. It is a time which places a spotlight on bonds, social encounters, and creating a sense of connection and belonging in your community. You reach completion of a significant journey, as the cycle comes full circle, you prepared to begin a new chapter of life. The past holds many memories of which you can treasure. It also has created a substantial growth and wisdom within you, this helps you plot a course which is in alignment with your higher goals, life works in profound ways. When you can tap into a deeper sense of awareness. This week speaks of letting go of an area which has blocked your progress, moving on to a new chapter of potential does give you the chance to better your situation. Reflecting on the past, provide you with insight and wisdom, this assists you on a journey of healing and resolving past areas which are best left behind. Trusting your inner voice does provide you with the right direction forward.

DECEMBER WEEK FOUR

Your life is entering an expansive phase, which sees your spirit soar. A golden era is coming, which has you team up with a kindred spirit. This takes you to new heights of adventure, and you are likely to go through a remarkable evolution which holds the potential to direct your path to an entirely new level.

Furthermore, this week is sentimental, you embrace fond memories of the past. It has given you the courage to overcome hurdles and achieve your highest outcome. You see a path towards greater security, and you are taking steps to manifest abundance in your life. Adding in goals does allow you to see tangible results which reflect the changes you are making in your life.

Additionally, this week is ruled by family ties, social gatherings, and lively discussions. Spending time with people you care about and share common interests with leaves you feeling rejuvenated. Seeing the beauty in your life enables you to gain perspective and release stress. You discover by the end of the week that you can revisit a long forgotten dream. This is something which creatively inspires, and you shall have luck on your side this time around. Your artistic side seeks expression. There are more serendipitous and inspirational moments ahead, and this shines a light on the area of healing and drawing joy into your world. You deserve a well-earned break, it's a time to give yourself space to just simply focus on nurturing your inner world.

Dear Stargazer,

I hope you have enjoyed planning your year with the stars utilizing Astrology and Zodiac influences. My zodiac star sign books are released each year which detail a monthly list of astrological events, and a weekly (four weeks to a month) horoscope. You can find more of my books at www.siasands.com

Feedback is welcomed and appreciated.

Many Blessings,

Sia Sands